W9-ASG-167
FEB 1971
RECEIVED
OHIO DOMINICAN
COLLEGE LIBRARY
COLUMBUS, OHIO
43219

UNIVERSITY OF MINNESOTA

PAMPHLETS ON AMERICAN WRITERS • NUMBER 73

Norman Mailer

BY RICHARD FOSTER

UNIVERSITY OF MINNESOTA PRESS · MINNEAPOLIS

Printed in the United States of America at
the North Central Publishing Co., St. Paul

Library of Congress Catalog Card Number: 68-64756

PUBLISHED IN GREAT BRITAIN, INDIA, AND PAKISTAN BY THE OXFORD UNIVERSITY PRESS, LONDON, BOMBAY, AND KARACHI, AND IN CANADA BY THE COPP CLARK PUBLISHING CO. LIMITED, TORONTO

FOR IRWIN AND WENDELL COREY

RICHARD FOSTER, a professor of English at Macalester College, is the author of *The New Romantics* and co-editor of *Modern Criticism: Theory and Practice.*

Norman Mailer

When Norman Mailer's *The Naked and the Dead* was published in 1948 it was all but universally acclaimed as a major novel marking the appearance of a new American writer destined for greatness. During the next twenty years, however, though he had some warm defenders, the negative judgments among critics substantially outnumbered the positive as book after book appeared: novels, a play, collections of stories and poems, and gatherings of essays and other fugitive pieces. And yet, unlike most of his generation of novelists – the "war novelists" and the urban Jewish writers – he has pursued a course of individualistic development and change which has continued to command the attention of peers, critics, and public; if his readers have sometimes been baffled and frequently hostile they have grown ever more interested. To use a Maileresque analogy, he has rather resembled an overmatched boxer who, floored in the second round, springs back and sustains the fight far beyond expectations through variety and inventiveness of footwork and temporizing punches.

The match is still not decided. But however it finally comes out, there can be no doubt that the overmatched boxer will at the very least be remembered for his remarkable performance. Mailer's adversary through the 1950's and 1960's has been the current embodiment of operative cultural and literary norms, that plodding but powerful opponent of idiosyncrasy and innovation which Eliot long ago dubbed "the tradition." Mailer had won his first round with a skillful and moving but conventional novel in the realist-naturalist vein. Everything since *The Naked and the Dead,* with the exception of a handful of stories from the late forties and early fifties, has been radically innovative in both substance and essential form—without satisfying current conceptions of what constitutes serious literary experimentation.

It has been Mailer's apparent lack of artistic "seriousness" that has troubled his serious critics most. When they were not either ridiculing or dismissing him, their main cry was the lamentation that a major talent was being wasted on trivial material or debased by sloppy craftsmanship. F. Scott Fitzgerald, whose work and career were in many ways similar to Mailer's, was criticized during his lifetime on much the same grounds. But what needs to be stressed in Mailer's case, as in Fitzgerald's, is that he is indeed a serious "experimentalist" writer, though an experimentalist of a different order than our moment in the history of "the tradition" allows us easily to recognize, accept, and understand.

James Joyce was the kind of experimentalist who applied innovative techniques to conventionally "realistic" fictional material. He sought out and found new routes to the old novelistic destinations. D. H. Lawrence, on the other hand, was the kind of writer who discovered new destinations—new materials and knowledge, and thus new obligations for fiction. His technical innovations, always less sophisticated, formal, and predominant than Joyce's, were functional consequences and by-products of what can only be called an experimentalist approach to the *subject matter* of fiction. In the course of writing *The Rainbow* and *Women in Love,* Lawrence discovered, as he told Edward Garnett, that his subject was no longer "the old stable *ego*" of human character, no longer the "diamond" but rather the "carbon" which is the diamond's elemental substance: "There is another *ego,* according to whose action the individual is unrecognisable, and passes through, as it were, allotropic states which it needs a deeper sense than any we've been used to exercise, to discover are states of the same single radically unchanged element. . . . Again I say, don't look for the development of the novel to follow the lines of certain characters: the characters fall into the form of some other rhythmic form, as when one draws a fiddle-bow across a fine tray delicately sanded, the sand takes lines unknown."

These metaphors describing the substantive nature of Lawrence's experimentation with both matter and form after *Sons and Lovers* might as easily apply to Mailer, whose work after *The Naked and the Dead* has been similarly concerned with the "allotropy" — the changing "rhythmic form" and "lines unknown" — of the "carbon" of human character under complex stress. And like Lawrence, Mailer seems to have become aware of his new departure only after standing away from the new work in hand to see what he was doing and why he was doing it. While working on *Barbary Shore*, he has recalled in an interview, he found his Marxist intellectual convictions continually distracted by compulsive preoccupations with "murder, suicide, orgy, psychosis." "I always felt as if I were not writing the book myself." Other statements by Mailer indicate that much the same creative pathology also ruled the composition of *The Deer Park*, his third novel. The personal stresses and anxieties that underlay the writing of these two novels, and the stories that were spun off from them, found confessional expression in Mailer's fourth book, a compilation of fiction and nonfiction pieces with unifying connective additions called *Advertisements for Myself*, which is the author's intense, immediate, and unabashedly public reappraisal of himself, in 1959, as both artist and human being. Anxiety, compulsion, and hints of psychosis had been the disruptive and only half-conscious creative causes behind *Barbary Shore* and *The Deer Park*. Following the purgation and illumination represented by *Advertisements* they become, in the later novels *An American Dream* and *Why Are We in Vietnam?* and the related pieces in *The Presidential*

Papers and *Cannibals and Christians,* the consciously molded substance of Mailer's hypertrophic images of life in America at mid-century.

A detailed account of this course of change and growth must be left for later. The important fact is that after several more books, plus a string of other accomplishments – including play-producing, movie-making, a fling at architectural design, and a great deal of moral, social, and political punditing, both on paper and on the hoof – the author of *The Naked and the Dead* emerged in the mid-sixties, despite his still uncertain reputation among serious literary people, as decidedly the most active and vivid public figure on the American literary scene.

Like his first published novel and stories, Mailer's early life was at least conventional enough not to foreshadow with any definiteness the panoply of idiosyncrasy that was to come later. Born January 31, 1923, in Long Branch, New Jersey, to Isaac and Fanny Mailer, Norman Mailer was raised and schooled in Brooklyn, graduating from Boys High School in 1939. While at Harvard, where he earned a B.S. degree in aeronautical engineering in 1943, Mailer began writing in earnest, contributing to the *Advocate,* working at his first two (and still unpublished) novels, and winning in 1941 *Story* magazine's annual college fiction contest. In 1944 he married his first wife and was drafted into the army, serving in the Pacific Theater until 1946. During the next year and a half, part of which was spent in Europe, where he was enrolled as a student at the Sorbonne, Mailer wrote *The Naked and the Dead,* which was published with immediate and dramatic success. The public purchased it in such numbers that it held at the top of the best-seller lists for nearly three months. A movie contract was soon in the works; Lillian Hellman was slated to adapt it for the stage; and Sinclair Lewis was moved to dub Mailer "the greatest writer to come out of his generation."

Though Mailer himself once half-dismissed his first novel as a "conventional war novel," and though it was conceived and composed in a manner that Mailer was not to use again in a major work, *The Naked and the Dead* is much more than a "war novel." The embracing action of the novel – the taking of a Japanese-held Pacific island in World War II – is rendered with the skilled realist's commitment to the truthful and vivid depiction of actuality. But in the year of its publication Mailer put on record his view that *The Naked and the Dead,* though cast in the realist mold, is "symbolic," expressive of "death and man's creative urge, fate, man's desire to conquer the elements – all kinds of things you never dream of separating and stating so baldly." And there is no mistaking that the island itself, and the mountain at its center which Sergeant Croft commits himself and his platoon to conquering, acquire an almost Conradian symbolic significance in the eyes of their chief beholders. Here is the soldiers' vision of the setting of their destruction:

It was a sensual isle, a Biblical land of ruby wines and golden sands and indigo trees. The men stared and stared. The island hovered before them like an Oriental monarch's conception of heaven, and they responded to it with an acute and terrible longing. It was a vision of all the beauty for which they had ever yearned, all the ecstasy they had ever sought. For a few minutes it dissolved the long dreary passage of the mute months in the jungle, without hope, without pride. If they had been alone they might have stretched out their arms to it.

It could not last. Slowly, inevitably, the beach began to dissolve in the encompassing night. The golden sands grew faint, became gray-green, and darkened. The island sank into the water, and the tide of night washed over the rose and lavender hills. After a little while, there was only the gray-black ocean, the darkened sky, and the evil churning of the gray-white wake. Bits of phosphorescence swirled in the foam. The black dead ocean looked like a mirror of the night; it was cold, implicit with dread and death. The men felt it absorb them in a silent pervasive terror. They turned back to their cots, settled down for the night, and shuddered for a long while in their blankets.

In an interview three years later, just after completing *Barbary Shore*, Mailer made this interesting disclosure about *The Naked and the Dead*: "I don't think of myself as a realist. That terrible word 'naturalism.' It was my literary heritage—the things I learned from Dos Passos and Farrell. I took naturally to it, that's the way one wrote a book. But I really was off on a mystic kick. Actually—a funny thing—the biggest influence on *Naked* was *Moby Dick*. . . . I was sure everyone would know. I had Ahab in it, and I suppose the mountain was Moby Dick. Of course, I also think the book will stand or fall as a realistic novel." This last qualification would also apply, of course, to *Moby Dick*. For Melville saw in the actual hazard and struggle of whaling, as Mailer did in war, the revealed pattern of the grandeur and tragedy of the whole human enterprise. Combat, for Mailer, is the chief means by which the higher laws of life become incarnate in human experience. War is his external subject matter in *The Naked and the Dead*; but his internal theme is the "crisis in human values"—identity, humanity, man, and the nature of their enemies in our time.

With war as the background typification of generalized external crisis, Mailer develops his internal themes by two principal means: first, extensively, through a number of Dos Passos-like diagnostic biographical portraits of a cross section of the fighting men; and second, intensively, through the protracted psychic struggle of mind and personality that takes place between Major General Cummings, the crypto-fascist commanding officer of the invading American forces, and his aide, a questioning liberal named Hearn. Both men have been shaped, though in opposite ways, by reaction against the privileged sterility of their midwestern bourgeois backgrounds. Cummings is the self-created prophet of a new totalitarianism who commands, in the name of his faith in order and authority, the breaking of men's spirits and the destruction of their wills. Hearn, bitter in his discontent, by nature a loner and yet tenderly humane in his half-guilty identification with the men he commands, is the uncertain voice of the liberal ideal of free man. Most of the fighting men are portrayed as already deprived, twisted, or stunted by the disintegrative and totalitarian forces and counterforces at work in their world, the forces whose contention has culminated in the war which now envelops them all. These men are the data of the dialectical contest which is taking place between Cummings and Hearn. That contest, the original of similar recurring patterns of individual contest, including sexual, in most of the rest of Mailer's work, ends in a kind of draw. Hearn and his convictions are wasted when he dies as a casual accident of war on an irrelevant mission. And though the campaign is won, Cummings is in essence defeated because the agency of victory is not his active military intelligence but rather a chain of chance accidents beyond his control.

One notices not only that a true hero is lacking from the novel's epic-like action, but that his opposite, a forceful antagonist, is lacking too. And yet a large enveloping energy has gathered, thrust forward, and come through to significant issue. A great spasm of nature, an inevitable motion of history, has superseded the efficacies of individual men in a world that has begun to move across Yeats's threshold of apocalypse where "the best lack all conviction" and "the worst/are full of passionate intensity."

But at the core of this vast action, his presence stressing the hero's absence, is Sergeant Croft. After the death of Hearn, he leads the platoon on its doomed assault upon the mountain, dominating his men by the sheer intensity of his undefined "hunger" for the mastery of life. A rough prototype of D. J. Jethroe of *Why Are We in Vietnam?*, Croft has been sired by a tough Texas dirt-farmer on a woman conventionally "weak . . . sweet and mild." His father encourages in him a predator's taste for hunting, and he is by nature "mean." Why? "Oh, there are answers. He is that way because of the corruption-of-the-society. He is that way because the devil has claimed him for one of his own. It is because he is a Texan; it is because he has renounced God." The author interprets Croft in an aside as follows: *"He hated weakness and he loved practically nothing. There was a crude unformed vision in his soul but he was rarely conscious of it."* This embryonic "vision" is different from Hearn's superannuated liberalism and Cummings' authoritarian calculus because it is an animal thing—an energy with fierce tendencies but no "form." Croft represents the kinetic life-substance upon which such alternative ideologies as those of Hearn and Cummings must depend for their unforeseeable realizations. In his irrational will and passion, he is the human microcosm of the vast upsurge of inhuman forces in history which express themselves in the ironic irresolutions of the total action of *The Naked and the Dead.*

The Naked and the Dead, then, even if substantially conventional in form and style, is nevertheless one with the rest of Mailer's work in the apocalyptic energies of its vision. Those energies begin to find their requisite new form, and with that a new sort of voice, in the first of Mailer's "experimental" novels, *Barbary Shore,* published in 1951. *Barbary Shore* was the product, as Mailer has written in retrospect, "of intense political preoccupation and a voyage in political affairs which began with the Progressive Party and has ended in the *cul-de-sac* (at least so far as action is concerned) of being an anti-Stalinist Marxist who feels that war is probably inevitable." The omniscient authorial point of view of *The Naked and the Dead* is abandoned in *Barbary Shore* for first-person narrative, which is to continue as the preferred narrative form for Mailer's books thereafter. ("Memory is the seed of narrative, yeah," says D. J. Jethroe, narrator of *Why Are We in Vietnam?*) The book becomes, thus, an adaptation of *Bildungsroman*; its narrative substance is the hero's education for life in our time – or re-education, since he is suffering from amnesia somewhat inexplicitly induced by war and the breakdown of traditional political idealism. The setting is a Brooklyn rooming house operated by a sexually promiscuous and morally neuter proprietress named, with an irony appropriate to her role as life's presiding norm, Guinevere. In this setting, the case histories of three roomers are presented: an impotent, betrayed, and self-betraying idealist of the old revolutionary left; his demon, a stolid and perverted interrogator for the rightist "totalitarian" establishment; and a mad Cassandra-like girl whose derangement is a consequence and expression of history, and whom, as an exacerbated mirroring of his own distressed psyche, the hero half loves.

The heaviness and inertia of the novel – its garrulous expositions of ideological conflict and the dazed passivity and blankness of Lovett, the hero-narrator, before all he sees and hears – is only a little relieved when at the end he sprints into an inchoate future with a mysterious small object entrusted to his keeping by the failed leftist before his death. The precise nature of the object, which is hotly coveted by the furies of the right, is never specified. But what it means is perfectly clear. It is a symbol or talisman of the sacred idea of man free and whole; and in the moment of the narrator's active commitment to it in the face of the terrible odds and enemies ranged against it, and now against him as well, we are meant to feel that it has taken on the existential power of life itself.

Even this early in his career – after only two novels – it is clear that Mailer's imagination, unique in his generation, is cast in the epic mold. As bard and prophet to an age in which history is at odds with nature or "destiny," he tells in a fevered voice of the permutations of the heroic imperative in a post-heroic world. His theme is the struggle of life and form against death and chaos. But his subject matter is history. And as he pursues the theme of the ideal through the matter of the actual he makes a discovery: in our time the sources and resources of life have shifted, to use the shorthand of Mailer's own symbology, from "God" to "the devil." The vision of life at stalemate in *The Naked and the Dead* and *Barbary Shore* is explained by this discovery, a discovery whose fullness of realization in a changed imaginative vision comes clear in *The Deer Park*, published in 1955.

Desert D'Or, a resort of the rich and powerful modeled on Palm Springs, is the principal setting of *The Deer Park*. It is a denatured interior world of concrete and plastic, of harsh light and blinding shadow, thrown up in defiance of the encircling desert outside. This pattern of division between natural and unnatural that is established in the setting extends also to the characters, in whom desire and will, feeling and thought, the wellsprings of motive and motive's fulfillment in action, have been stricken apart. The natural current of the life-force has somehow been broken. And the inhabitants of this world of trauma and aftermath constitute a gallery of parodies of the human image ranging from the absurd to the piteous to the monstrous. They are, as Mailer wrote in a note to his adaptation of *The Deer Park* for the stage, "in hell."

Sergius O'Shaugnessy, the hero-narrator of *The Deer Park*, is both an orphan and, like Lovett of *Barbary Shore*, a symbolic waif of historical disaster. His surrogate home in the air force and fulfillment in the exercise of the war pilot's impersonal skills of destruction have been snatched from him in a sudden accidental revelation that he is a killer: "I realized that . . . I had been busy setting fire to a dozen people, or two dozen, or had it been a hundred?" In recoil from such horrors of the "real world" he suffers a breakdown, is discharged, and on the winnings from a prodigiously lucky gambling venture, he comes to Desert D'Or, retreat of the gods of the "imaginary world," to rest, drift, gaze, and spend. A blank slate to be written on, an empty vessel to be filled, and—his vision of the burned flesh of his victims having rendered him sexually impotent—a low flame needing fuel, Sergius O'Shaugnessy is the framing consciousness of an ample world crowded with people exhibiting versions of his own predicament. Among the most important of these are Charles Francis Eitel, a gifted and formerly powerful Hollywood director, and Marion Faye, dope pusher, impressario of call girls, and connoisseur of the moral nuances of sadism. Both of these men become friends of O'Shaugnessy and objects of his studious moral attention.

Eitel has had a golden age, a brief heroic period in the thirties when as a true artist he made courageous movies on contemporary social themes, and when as a man of integrity he put his life on the line in behalf of the fated struggle for democracy in Spain. In reflexive response to the corruption of integrity which has overtaken his art as he has risen to power in Hollywood, Eitel rebuffs a congressional investigating committee seeking from him incriminating political testimony against his colleagues. In consequence, the industry blackballs him; and his loss of power and identity in the "imaginary" world is measured in personal terms by his loss of potency as both artist and lover. This sequential pattern of aspiration, action, corruption, moral illumination, renunciation, exile, and impotence precisely parallels the pattern of Sergius' life. Eitel is the distillate of the best values of the past by which Sergius has been fathered and orphaned, and for Sergius, consequently, the question of Eitel's destiny—the question of his potential for rebirth and self-renewal—has crucial moral significance.

Eitel stumbles upon a "second chance" in the form of Elena Esposito, and he muffs it. Another man's castoff, she is soiled, tawdry, and simple. She is a poor dancer and a worse actress, and her manners are absurd. And yet she has the dignity and courage, and finally the beauty, of a being wholly natural. Eitel's affair with her becomes the nourishing ground of a new life for him. His sexual potency is restored, and with it his creative potency as he begins to work on a script which he imagines will be the redemption of his integrity as artist and man. But this new access of life fills him with fear; it is the stirring in him of the heroic imperative, with its attendant commitments to solitary battle, lonely journeyings in the unknown, and the risks of failure and defeat. The doors of Hollywood begin to open again, and the thrones and dominations of the "imaginary" world solicit his return: all he must do is confess and recant before the committee, and he may pass back through those doors. Half because of fear, half because of old habit, Eitel takes the easy way of surrender, shunning the hazardous alternatives (as Elena, significantly, does not) represented by those dark angels of life and truth, Don Beda, high priest of satyrism and orgy, and Marion Faye, the hipster prophet of criminal idealism. His harvest is the life-in-death of security through compromise, the corruption of his script and his talent, and eventual marriage to a broken and exhausted Elena, which is possible now that they are no longer "wedded" in a sacramental sense.

Elena is a noble figure — defeated, but honorably so, in her fated but heroic contest with time and what Hardy calls "crass casualty." Eitel's enemies have been lesser ones — history and social circumstance — and his defeat is pitiful rather than noble, because he has "sold out." But he has at least the saving grace of his ironic intelligence, which enables him to understand, when she proudly refuses his first offer of marriage, the principle of Elena's nobility: "the essence of spirit . . . was to choose the thing which did not better one's position but made it more perilous." Later on, when she has no more resources of refusal and he nourishes upon her defeat by "sacrificing" himself in marrying her, he understands his own corresponding cowardice: "there was that law of life so cruel and so just which demanded that one must grow or else pay more for remaining the same."

Eitel is Mailer's version of the traditional hero in his last historical incarnation. Vision, passion, and courage have dwindled in Eitel to intelligence, compassion, and guilt – the "cement" of the world, as Marion Faye contemptuously labels the last two, which binds men, enfeebles them, and turns them into spiritual "slobs." Eitel's very strengths are weaknesses, his virtues are faults, in a world where the apocalyptic beasts of anxiety and dread are raging in prisons of compromise and falsehood. And as the novel draws to its close and Eitel begins to fade into the penumbra of Sergius O'Shaugnessy's memorializing imagination, we are aware that the passing of the man is also the passing of the values he represented. Flanked by comic Lulu Meyers, a movie sex goddess who on impulse marries for "love" rather than career, and by tragic Marion Faye whose anarch's code of black moral reason leads him behind prison bars, the now enlightened Sergius is the chief chalice-bearer of new human values. He becomes a bullfighter, stud, and teacher of both arts. And he begins to write, his books presumably fired by the existential perils and ecstasies of combat and sexuality. Though the novel ends on a cheerful note of metaphysical exhilaration, Sergius, both as a character and as an archetype of new styles of human value, is vague and inchoate as well as faintly absurd. Sergius has survived all sorts of traumas and temptations and come through to freedom, but he is not very much more fully realized as an examplar of new values in action than was his predecessor, Lovett. He has come to terms with the world that has wounded him, and like the good Emersonian "fatalists" that all such Mailer heroes are, he affirms it as his destined inheritance from nature and history. But neither he nor his author has yet found the requisite life-style, the new heroic mold through which to turn understanding and affirmation into creative, perhaps redemptive action.

Life threatened in our time by the forces of death is Mailer's subject everywhere. When he writes as a realist, as in *The Naked and the Dead,* life is stalemated and defeated by the forces of death. In the next two novels the intensities of anxiety and dread underlying Mailer's subject matter begin to dominate the rational, circumjacent forms of the realist, distorting them in the direction of the expressionistic and the surreal. And with this modification of form comes a coordinate modification of the heroes in whom the issue of the life-death struggle is finally centered. The narrator-hero of *Barbary Shore,* for whom the action encompassed by his consciousness is an elaborately instructive morality play, in the end escapes paralysis and spiritual death. The similarly educated narrator-hero of *The Deer Park* not only escapes but, as he bids fond farewell to the memories of the defeated and destroyed, discerns in the very chemistry of the disease and decomposition all around him the flicker and spur of new possibilities for life. "Think of Sex as Time," says "God" in a final dialogue with Sergius, "and Time as the connection of new circuits."

Barbary Shore and *The Deer Park,* both of them fictional investigations of the operative laws of death and endings, are novels that end with beginnings. Mailer's next novel, *An American Dream,* published in 1965, is in every way an extension and intensification of the manner and substance of its two predecessors. It begins, significantly, with an ending: the hero saves himself from spiritual death by committing a murder that restores him to life, action, growth. Seen in relation to *An American Dream,* the two preceding novels have the look of a single imaginative action of a precursory nature: a complex psycho-dramatic "sloughing-off," to use Lawrence's terms in *Studies in Classic American Literature,* of the "old consciousness" of an outworn idealistic humanism in preparation for a "new consciousness" requisite for survival and significant life in a psychotic world bordering on apocalypse and yearning toward death. The experiential educations of Mikey Lovett and Sergius O'Shaugnessy in *Barbary Shore* and *The Deer Park* are preparations of this "new consciousness" for active engagement with the world. Steve Rojack and D. J. Jethroe – respectively heroes of *An American Dream* and *Why Are We in Vietnam?* – are the beneficiaries of this process. Rojack, in a moment of freeing impulse, murders his rich, preternaturally domineering, death-threatening wife Deborah, a "bitch-goddess" of American power, and the summation of the death-force of historical fate. The charge of this self-galvanizing destruction of his immediate enemy propels him into action, turning fear, fatigue, and despair into a redemptive energy of desperation. With a courage nourished on the ultimate dread, the dread of death, he runs a varied course of triumphs – besting the sexual enmity of a cold nymphomaniac, the hunting wile of the police, the competition of a Negro stud of legendary sexual prowess, and an engulfing sea of guilt and self-doubt summoned by Deborah's father, Barney Kelly. He even finds love along the way, with a tender, used, and charming cabaret singer named Cherry. A composite of American realities like Deborah, she is Deborah's opposite and complement, a plucky victim of the forces of which Deborah is the emblematic goddess and proprietress. At the end Rojack is still running – his roles and costumes of war hero, congressman, professor, television personality, and husband of a socialite left far behind – now toward the darker and simpler challenges of the jungles of Guatemala and Yucatán.

In *Why Are We in Vietnam?* (1967), D. J. Jethroe has already reached his Guatemala and Yucatán. High on pot, the prose of the Marquis de Sade and William Burroughs, and the cheerfully psychotic inspiration that he may be the voice of a "Harlem spade" imprisoned in the body of the son of a white Dallas tycoon, he tells the story of how he got that way. It is an initiation story (new style) as *An American Dream* was a new-style story of sacrifice and redemption. The initiation, product of a hunting "safari" to Alaska with his father Rusty, D. J.'s best friend Tex, and assorted guides and associates, has two phases, both of them involving radical divestments and ultimate tests of courage. In the first phase, D. J. breaks spiritually with his father when, out of habits of competitive vanity and self-justification, his father claims the grizzly bear that D. J. has mortally wounded, violating not only the father-son bond as reinforced by the hunt (stalking their dangerous quarry D. J. sees himself and his father as "war buddies") but also the sacred blood bond between killer and prey. Thinks D. J., "Final end of love of one son for one father." The second phase of the initiation, fruit of the alienation and frustration sown by the first, is the twenty-four-hour northward foray of D. J. and Tex, alone and without guns or instruments, into the wild heart of the Brooks Range. In an ecstasy of fear and trembling they witness a pageant of savageries – wolf, eagle, bear, caribou, and moose, the figments of natural life locked in struggle with death – culminating in a cosmic eruption of the Northern Lights that is so magnificent and intense as to bring them to the border of orgy and fratricide: "they were twins, never to be as lovers again, but killer brothers, armed by something, prince of darkness, lord of light, they did not know." They make a bond in an exchange of blood, "the deep beast whispering, Fulfill my will, go forth and kill." At the end, D. J., now eighteen, looks beyond the Brooks Range of his initiatory "Guatemala and Yucatán" toward his mature destiny: "Hot damn, Vietnam."

D. J. is the voice of the anxieties and compulsions that have accumulated beneath the patterns of America's history and exploded at last in the manifest violence and chaos of its present. In the electric North, which is the voltaic pile of a continent's repressed, distorted, and perverted life-energies, he has faced Demogorgon, and he comes back metamorphosed, a rudely American voice of bardic ecstasy and prophecy. Completing the journey of transformation only begun by Lovett and Sergius O'Shaugnessy, D. J. and Steve Rojack have successfully tracked the power of life, thieved by a conspiracy of history with nature from its traditional home in the light, to its new home in darkness. In accomplishing this, they become exemplars of that "new consciousness" requisite to continuing life's ancient battle against death in a psychotic world bordering on apocalyptic crisis.

Richard Poirier, identifying Mailer with Eliot's vision, sees him as similarly spurred by the "de-creative" aspects of creation. But if this is true, Mailer is even more closely related to Lawrence, who in the voice of Rupert Birkin of *Women in Love* discerned among the "marsh-flowers" of "destructive creation" certain blossoms that while they were spawned by the all-enveloping historical process of "universal dissolution" were not "*fleurs du mal*," but rather "roses, warm and flamy." Lawrence himself was one of these exotic exceptions. And so is Mailer. If the roots of both writers necessarily nourish upon the food of darkness, the blossoms produced are bright with the warm colors of life, and grow toward the light. In Lawrence the blossom is the "man who has come through," the separate natural self released through the death of the conventional social self into a living and changing "star-equilibrium" with the otherness of nature and woman. In Mailer it is all this and a bit more: history, impelled by the American dream turned to nightmare, is a third constituent of the otherness, and the reborn self becomes an "existential hero."

Advertisements for Myself (1959) and *The Presidential Papers* (1963) are large and various but nevertheless unified collections of pieces, mostly nonfiction, written during the dozen years following Mailer's tentative effort and partial failure to achieve a new form in *Barbary Shore*. As books principally about their author, *Advertisements for Myself* and *The Presidential Papers* taken together have the shape, like *Barbary Shore* and *The Deer Park*, of a single action, the complex and difficult action of "sloughing off" the "old consciousness." "The existential hero," first coming to full life in *An American Dream* and *Why Are We in Vietnam?*, is Mailer's realization of this new style of consciousness. And *Advertisements for Myself* and *The Presidential Papers* are the record of its gestation in the mind of its creator, and of the large and small deaths prerequisite to its coming to birth.

Mailer uses his own "personality," he tells us, as the "armature" of *Advertisements* – an image aptly descriptive of both its form and its impact. The reciprocal emotions of dread and determination whirl at the center of the book, as its author frankly appraises, at mid-career, his qualified victories and larger defeats during more than a decade of trying to live up to his potentials and ambitions as a man and writer. The pieces collected in *Advertisements* – stories, essays, and poems; polemics, meditations, and interviews; fragments of plays-in-progress and novels-to-be – are the measure of the worth of the life being lived, the substance of the tale being told. It is a tale, like Fitzgerald's in "The Crack-Up" essays, of early success, subsequent failure and demoralization, and the reflexive counterthrust of self-regeneration and re-creation. *The Naked and the Dead*, which catapulted him to sudden and youthful fame, had, as he tells us in *Advertisements*, been "easy to write." But nothing would be so easy again, for this success was the beginning of his "existentialism," which was "forced upon [him]," as he says, by his finding himself "prominent and empty," a "personage," at twenty-five. He must justify the prominence and fill the emptiness. With such heroic models before him as the lifestyle of Hemingway and the *oeuvre* of Malraux, he thrusts experimentally into new territory with *Barbary Shore*, "the first of the existentialist novels in America." The hostility and ridicule with which it is greeted in 1951 knock him down. Deflated, ill, and anxious, he turns to writing "respectable" short stories in the earlier manner and jaunty socio-political polemics for such magazines as *Partisan Review* and *Dissent* (of which he also becomes an editor). All this is a sort of distraction and temporizing in the face of the big comeback, the planned colossal counterpunch which might dazzle the world with a starfall and revelations: a projected eight-volume novel of cosmic proportions whose framing consciousness, a minor man and an artist *manqué* named Sam Slovoda, has an alter ego dream-hero named Sergius O'Shaugnessy. The great work hovering in the wings refuses to emerge. But two related fragments appear, both of them again in the new manner: the story "The Man Who Loved Yoga," which is to be the great work's prologue, and a protracted but relevant detour from the main route, a novel called *The Deer Park.*

The story of the vicissitudes accompanying *The Deer Park*'s publication and reception, most of it recounted in *Advertisements,* could itself be the stuff of a novel. The bad reception of *Barbary Shore* in 1951 and Mailer's divorce in 1952 are elements of a continuing pattern of gathering personal distress which characterize the years of *The Deer Park*'s composition. These distresses reach a penultimate crisis when *The Deer Park,* already in page proof, is suddenly held up by its publisher: Stanley Rinehart finds in it something unacceptably obscene. Just recently Mailer has accepted the challenge of writing an essay called "The Homosexual Villain" at the invitation of the magazine *One,* an undertaking which has blown up a "log jam of accumulated timidities and restraints" in him. Partially as a consequence, he refuses to make the change in *The Deer Park* for Rinehart, and the deal is off. The next ten weeks, at the end of which *The Deer Park* will be accepted by Putnam after refusal by several other houses, is a time of crisis for Mailer. He has undergone another death – the death of certain illusions about himself as "a figure in the landscape," and about the "honor" of publishers and writers in the American present – and feels himself becoming a "psychic outlaw."

Drawing his powers now from forays into the worlds of jazz, Harlem, and marijuana, he sees that the style of *The Deer Park* is wrong for the narrator he wants to create – it is too poetic, in the vein of Fitzgerald's Nick Carraway. He begins to rewrite from page proof, thirsting for the kind of self-redemptive success which would change the world a little, and at the same time dreading the possibility of a bad reception and low sales. The revised *The Deer Park,* once published, is only a "middling success." And Mailer measures the quality of its success not only by sales and reviews but by the glimpses of possibility that have begun to emerge for the harried author with his last-minute impetus to rewrite it. Though tentative and incomplete, the accomplished changes adumbrate a new hero: the tender, wounded, and detached observer of the earlier version has begun to turn into a Sergius O'Shaugnessy who is not only "good" but also "ambitious"; a Sergius who, instead of virtuously spurning Hollywood's offer to film his life, might have taken the bait in a spirit of adventure and run it to some perilous triumph. The published book, its author laments, is but a hint of what might have been: the masterpiece in Mailer's generation equivalent to *The Sun Also Rises* in Hemingway's. As a "middling success," *The Deer Park* represents to its author his gross failure to bid on "the biggest hand" he had ever held, and a discovery that after all he hadn't the magic to "hasten the time of apocalypse."

But even so, this fumble, this failure, is no dead end. Like the emptiness of his success with *The Naked and the Dead,* and the fullness of his failure with *Barbary Shore,* it is a threshold to possibility. He has a vision, now, of what he must try to be and do as a writer, and of how considerable are the odds ranged against him. And like Sergius, who takes up bullfighting at the end of *The Deer Park*, he moves directly into the arena of the world's action as a matador of existential polemics—a rebel general of "Hip"—in the pages of *The Village Voice*, which he helped found in 1955. Though a fresh excursion into novel-writing is delayed by these side trips into journalism, *The Village Voice* pieces are important as snapshots of the "new" Mailer soon fully to emerge as exemplar and spokesman of the needed "new consciousness." His first important effort in the new mode is the essay *The White Negro*, written in 1957 and first published, by City Lights, in 1958 (it was reprinted in *Advertisements*).

A speculative psycho-cultural essay on the modern predicament, *The White Negro* is a paradigm of the vision, the ideas, the motifs and symbols that will shape all of Mailer's future work in whatever form. The Hipster refuses to capitulate to the repressive denaturing, dehumanizing death-force of a "totalitarian" society. But because he is active—unlike the bourgeois "beat" who withdraws and passively sublimates in the surrogate quasi-life of song, flowers, meditation, hallucinogens, and "love"—he is confronted by the immediate dangers of physical violence and death. Like the Negro he is an *un*citizen (hence the label "white Negro") and danger is the medium of his life. Pleasure is his end; energy, courage, and wile are his means. The dynamic poise of his life-style implies the constitution, in microcosm, of a whole culture: decorums of manners, dress, language; an ethic; an aesthetic; even, finally, a metaphysic and a theology. The philosophy of the Hip, Mailer reflects, is the formed insight of a "radical humanist" "brooding" on the energizing phenomenon of the Negro revolution in contemporary America.

The Hipster is, of course, only one of many possible realizations of the "new consciousness" of which Mailer is the prophet. He is but one version of the idea of the existential hero, whose incarnation not only *may* but *must* be limitless and unpredictable. For the existential hero is the Dostoevskian underground man come aboveground into the Tolstoian mainstream of history. It is not known what he will be there, only that he will *do*—his being a function of his acting, rather than the other way around. He is a Sisyphus released from the stone of his dogged abstract commitment, a Hemingway galvanized into new life by the very terrors that threaten paralysis and death. Evading the fateful impasse between heroic "intactness" and human "completeness" that destroyed Fitzgerald's Dick Diver, he is a vital synthesis of the polar values of self-control and spontaneity represented in *The Deer Park* by Marion Faye, the black puritan of moral scruple, and Don Beda, the rosy orgiast of the senses. Extensively educated in anguish, division, and impotence, Sergius O'Shaugnessy has just touched the regenerative power of that synthesis when the book of his salvation closes. The same efflorescence in his creator, which achieves full bloom in *The Presidential Papers,* seems to have been nourished by a similar curriculum, as recounted in *Advertisements,* of prior defeats and despairs. *Advertisements,* in contrast to its successor, *The Presidential Papers,* is a book in the mode of elegy, recording in lyric regret and anger the difficult passing of romantic idealism and the death of youth's illusions. But *Advertisements* also has elegy's *dramatic* mode, being shaped as a total action embodying patterns of divestment and purgation which yield up at last a clear prospect of fresh possibilities: "Tomorrow to fresh woods, and pastures new." *The White Negro,* which Mailer tells us was written in the depths of "fear that I was no longer a writer," turns out to be the bright and central song of a "man who has come through." It is after all, he sees, one of his "best things." In it, and in the two late stories in the "existential" mode, "The Time of Her

Time" and "Advertisements for Myself on the Way Out," published at the close of *Advertisements,* can be found, as he says, "the real end of this muted autobiography of the near-beat adventurer who was myself."

The end of a life, whether well or badly lived, Mailer writes in *Advertisements,* is "seed." The "seed" of the agonies survived by the hero of *Advertisements* is *The Presidential Papers,* in which the author steps forth, re-created as public man and existentialist prophet, to address America and its leaders on the exigent realities of the age.

The "armature" of this book is not the author's personality in crisis, but rather an *idea* – the idea of "existential politics": "Existential politics is simple. It has a basic argument: if there is a strong ineradicable strain in human nature, one must not try to suppress it or anomaly, cancer and plague will follow. Instead one must find an art into which it can grow." In *The Presidential Papers* the pattern of personal crisis and salvation of self traced in *Advertisements* has been transmuted, by the chemistry of analogy so characteristic of Mailer's imagination, into the public terms of politics and history. But though the drama is now public rather than private, Mailer's self is no less central to the action. In the preface to *The Presidential Papers* he defines his role: to infuse John F. Kennedy, whose glamour and magnetism give him the potential of an "existential hero" in the arena of politics, with the requisite "existential" political consciousness. Mailer's commitment here is to steal back, for the languishing forces of "God," some of the energies of life which have passed over to the forces of darkness. But because history has moved so far on the downward path of de-creation, he must do it as a kind of undercover agent: he must perforce speak as a "devil." His first success as a metaphysical Robin Hood is his brilliant *Esquire* piece on Kennedy's nomination by the 1960 Democratic convention, which was written, despite his candidate's moribund "liberal" program, for the purpose of getting this rare man, so blessed "with a face," elected. For it is Mailer's belief that this essay, a product of his "Faustian" pact with "Mephisto," was the generative cause of Kennedy's small plurality over Nixon in the election. The rest of *The Presidential Papers* is a contemporaneous critique (with the blood, sweat, and tears of immediate response staining the pages) of "the Kennedy years," that ambiguous and perhaps despair-making hisorical return on its author's original existential wager.

Of all the fine pieces following, perhaps the most memorable is the essay on the Patterson-Liston fight, subtitled "Death." This essay is many things: It is a skillful piece of evocative journalism about an actual event; a symbolist's reading of the forces at war in the submerged psyche of America; a strange, oblique prophesy, through a poet's analysis of the attrition and inevitable doom of the spirit of American liberal idealism, of Kennedy's assassination. It is also a gaily profound exploration of the absurdity, and perhaps the peril, awaiting the writer as performing tragic-comedian whose ambition is to ride at the same time both bright Pegasus and the dark horses of wrath. But if the end — or "seed" — of life is life itself, then that effort must be made in spite of all hazard: "To believe the impossible may be won," Mailer writes elsewhere in *The Presidential Papers,* "creates a strength from which the impossible may be attacked." And in our time, though the memory of "God" and the light may shape ultimate heroic purpose, the hero draws nourishment for his "humanism" (a favorite recurring word of Mailer's) from the devil's realm, venturing ever more deeply — as Mailer does in the barbarous poems and scatological dialogues collected in *Cannibals and Christians* — into the territories of darkness.

Cannibals and Christians, published in 1966, is not so good a book as its two omnibus predecessors, though it has its bright spots, such as the piece on Goldwater's nomination and the temptation it wakens in its author to ride this newest bandwagon of the devil. The drama of self-discovery and re-creation, which gave unity to the brilliance and variety of *Advertisements* and *Papers,* is slowed and muffled in *Cannibals* by the didactic accents of the guru who gazes upon a vision that is cooling toward dogma and repetition. But it is perhaps understandable that the imaginative breakthrough represented by *An American Dream* should be followed by a somewhat studious contemplation of the truths revealed, for something more than half of the stuff of *Cannibals* was written shortly after *Dream.* Mailer himself seems to be aware of the condition. Written in a time of "plague" and under a lurid cloud of apocalyptic expectations, the collection is concerned with themes, he says, more appropriate to a novel. He feels again the impulse to "go back to that long novel, announced six years ago, and changed in the mind by all of seven years." *Cannibals,* he reflects, may be the last such collection for a while.

Since *Cannibals,* in addition to publishing *Why Are We in Vietnam?* Mailer has produced off Broadway his dramatization of *The Deer Park,* a crisply successful play in which a much clearer and more effective Sergius O'Shaugnessy has been purchased at the expense of the novel's richly internal realization of Eitel and Elena. He has also directed, produced, and starred in two full-length "existential" films of his own conceiving. The requisite honors have begun, belatedly, to come his way: in 1967 he was elected to the National Institute of Arts and Letters. And in October of the same year, this author of twelve books, father of six children, and veteran of four wives — "heroines all," he has gallantly affirmed — proved his continued interest in the public life of his time by getting himself arrested, jailed, and fined for an act of civil disobedience in the great Washington demonstrations against the war in Vietnam.

The immediate result of this was *The Armies of the Night,* published in the spring of 1968, a kind of autobiographical novel with a protagonist called "Mailer" who is at once an absurd citizen of "technology-land" in crisis and a bard of the bright dream that lies behind the thickening miasmas of the betrayed and perishing republic. It is unquestionably one of Mailer's best books – passionate, humorous, acutely intelligent, and, as always, eloquent in its empathy with the drift of history. It has new riches in it, too, of a more incidental kind, such as a gallery of sharply intimate verbal cartoons, highlighted with the reflected pigments of Mailer's own uniquely anxious self-image, of such primary men of our moment as Robert Lowell, Dwight Macdonald, and Paul Goodman. But most striking of all are its undercurrents of a softer emotion than we have been used to finding in Mailer, a new tenderness for life that lets him muse warmly along the way on his troubled love for his wife, his children, his mythic America. There is even a touch of nostalgic religious craving in it, a small recurring thirst for "Christ." But though the texture of feeling is more varied, the old Mailer, familiarly gravid with the epic furies and ambitions of a diminutive Brooklyn Achilles, still prevails:

> Mailer, looking back, thought bitter words he would not say: "You, Lowell, beloved poet of many, what do you know of the dirt and the dark deliveries of the necessary? What do you know of dignity hard-achieved, and dignity lost through innocence, and dignity lost by sacrifice for a cause one cannot name? What do you know about getting fat against your will, and turning into a clown of an arriviste baron when you would rather be an eagle or a count, or rarest of all, some natural aristocrat from these damned democratic states? No, the only subject we share, you and I, is that species of perception which shows that if we are not very loyal to our unendurable and most exigent inner light, then some day we may burn. How dare you condemn me! . . . How dare you scorn the explosive I employ?"

Lowell falls backward at this moment in the narrative, a noble Hector going bump on his head, as if toppled by the lightning bolt of his adversary's thought. Though *The Armies of the Night* is tempered with new softnesses and warmths, such passages would deter one from concluding too easily that Mailer may be getting ready to write his hymn of reconciliation – his *Tempest* or "Lapis Lazuli," his *Billy Budd* or *Old Man and the Sea.*

Good as *The Armies of the Night* is, and prolific in a variety of media as Mailer has been in the last decade, the great opus so long ago announced remains unachieved. Are such varied and frequent detours from the high road of novel-writing threatening, at this prime of his creative life, the ultimate dissipation of Mailer's talent as a major writer? This already familiar question was raised yet again by an interviewer in *Playboy* for January 1968. Mailer answered that the pattern of his career was dictated by his instinctive feeling that "the best way to grow was not to write one novel after another but to move from activity to activity, a notion that began with Renaissance man." He does not mention the example of Milton, but he might as well have. Then, coming down off the high horse of the moment's rhetoric, he adds genially, "It's not my idea, after all."

He is, of course, right both about himself and about "the tradition." With the romantic movement the imaginative writer became alienated from public life. Next, under the neoclassical reactive pressure of modernist formalism, he became in a sense alienated even from his work – which was not to be an utterance but an object, a product of the "impersonal" operations of imagination. With this background in view, it is clear that Mailer's uniqueness as a mid-century writer lies in his conscious cultivation, in the manner of Yeats, of a dynamic interrelation between his art and his life-style. Intensely himself, he is nevertheless the writer reborn in the dimension of public man. Engorged with the inclusive themes of his age and his nation, his work is nevertheless deeply personal. "I've been working on one book most of my life," he told the *Playboy* interviewer. "Probably since I started with *Barbary Shore,* certainly with and since *The Deer Park,* I've been working on one book." As he tells us in the introduction to *Cannibals and Christians,* he is, like Lawrence, Henry Miller, and Hemingway, writing "one continuing book . . . of [his] life and the vision of [his] existence." He might also have mentioned Fitzgerald whom he resembles in this respect as well as in many others, including his sense of the integral relation between the moral health of the artist and the quality of his art conceived as "style." "A really good style," said Mailer in his *Paris Review* interview of 1964, as if in echo of a dozen similar testimonies by Fitzgerald, "comes only when a man has become as good as he can be. Style is character."

"Style," broadly understood as the individual humane stance a writer chooses to take in relation to his material along its whole spectrum from language to vision, is perhaps the judgmental critic's most useful tool in approaching such a writer. For both the strengths and weaknesses of Mailer's work are the products of his unique commitment to being as "good," and thus as creative, a man as he can.

As recently as the early sixties, fairly literate people – often critics and teachers – were still saying that though Mailer certainly had a novelist's gift he "couldn't write." He was in their minds a kind of James Jones who, with no appropriate arsenal of sophistication, had gone adventuring into frontier territories of the imagination and was never heard of again. "I can't read him any more," they would say; and it was at least evident that these people who made themselves responsible for keeping up with Bellow and Malamud, Styron and Barth – current writers favored with recognition by the critical establishment – *weren't* reading him, whether or not they *couldn't* read him. To them he was at once nuttier than D. H. Lawrence, dumber than Sinclair Lewis, artistically more unselective even than Thomas Wolfe, these faults clumsily wrapped in a style a good deal more wooden and awkward than Dreiser's. Because they weren't reading him it wasn't possible to argue with any hope of success that his "beliefs" were the poetical vehicles of a metaphysician's speculative insights; that he was the only important novelist on the American scene who was also an authentic and sophisticated intellectual; that if he was temperamentally the inclusive artist, he was also deftly capable of the lean and compact virtuoso performance; and that his style — ranging the spectrum from slang to sublimity — was a distillate of all the rest into a shimmering and variegated brilliancy of words. An example from *The Armies of the Night*:

There was an aesthetic economy to symbolic gestures — you must not repeat yourself. Arrested once, TV land would accept him (conceivably) as a man willing to stand up for his ideas; get busted twice on the same day, and they would view him as a freak-out panting for arrest. (Mailer's habit of living — no matter how unsuccessfully — with his image, was so ingrained by now, that like a dutiful spouse he was forever consulting his better half.)

This is the style incisive, the author cutting an idea down to the gem of epigram at its center. An example from *The Presidential Papers*:

It is the wisdom of a man who senses death within him and gambles that he can cure it by risking his life. It is the therapy of the instinct, and who is so wise as to call it irrational? Before he went into the Navy, Kennedy had been ailing. Washed out of Freshman year at Princeton by a prolonged trough of yellow jaundice, sick for a year at Harvard, weak already in the back from an injury at football, his trials suggest the self-hatred of a man whose resentment and ambition are too large for his body. Not everyone can discharge their furies on an analyst's couch, for some angers can be relaxed only by winning power, some rages are sufficiently monumental to demand that one try to become a hero or else fall back into that death which is already within the cells. But if one succeeds, the energy aroused can be exceptional. . . . One thinks of that three-mile swim with the belt in his mouth and McMahon holding it behind him. There are pestilences which sit in the mouth and rot the teeth – in those five hours how much of the psyche must have been remade, for to give vent to the bite in one's jaws and yet use that rage to save a life: it is not so very many men who have the apocalyptic sense that heroism is the First Doctor. . . . With such a man in office the myth of the nation would again be engaged . . .

This is the style progenitive, the author pushing out from the central root-and-trunk idea a branch-bud-and-leaf exfoliation of confirmatory images.

Mailer's style is a style of eddying gusts and pointed audible silences textured on a background of the musing, ruminating, wondering human voice. Voice is the style's medium; its creative means are the instrumentalities of wit and amplification. Its end is to disclose, through dynamic interplay of the reciprocal rhetorics of incision and proliferation, the submerged realities of experience. Through implosion and explosion of the facts and patterns of common life, it intends to force a new vision upon the reader – to transform him, galvanize him, free him to become the vehicle of apocalypse. It is predictable that an imagination so metaphysically ambitious as Mailer's should generate fictions which, though open-ended and loosely shaped, contain a dense internal unity of interlocking analogies, and that that unity should be mirrored in a prose coordinately dense with analogizing metaphor.

Mailer's style of imagination is a *forcing* style: it exerts *force* upon reality; it seeks to *force* reality into the matrix of an idiosyncratic vision. This *urgency* is the key to Mailer's most prominent strengths: the relentless energy of desperation which makes *An American Dream* a single breathless action, and gathers the many moods and modes of *Advertisements* into a sharply unified portrait of the artist as a young man fighting the demons of crack-up; the monumentality of certain of his chief theme-bearing characters – John F. Kennedy and Herman Teppis, Sonny Liston and Deborah Kelly Rojack – who remain in the memory as vivid larger-than-life creatures of myth; and the fluency everywhere, from the close, sharp lash of the goading scatologist to the barrel-toned magniloquence of the bard.

But these strengths are shadowed by related weaknesses: a dulling of awareness through a persistence in urgency that is too relentless; a flatness, stockness, vagueness in characterization often, when the fictionist in the author inevitably capitulates to the didact; and a tendency to flatulence, garrulousness, clotted heaviness, that threatens to choke the naturally vigorous life of the prose. One is irritated, and finally deafened, by the sado-masochistic acid-head bebop and chowder mannerisms of D. J. Jethroe's nonstop answer to the question Why Are We in Vietnam? – though there are "good things" in this work, and tightened up it might have made a memorable short story or novella. Sergius O'Shaugnessy is disastrously vague, and Marion Faye is flat; their central moral significance in *The Deer Park* is diminished to abstraction and formula by their failure to be as human as the roundly conceived moral cripples surrounding them in the populous world of Desert D'Or. (Collie Munshin is a pretty bloom of humanity by comparison.) And the ingenious dialogues on the metaphysics of death and excrement in *The Presidential Papers* and *Cannibals and Christians* are, when all is said and done, overextended and boring. And boring is, of course, one of the most undesirable things you can be in the Mailer canon of humane values. These qualities represent a temptation perhaps innate to Mailer's kind of sensibility. In *The Armies of the Night*, for example, he is attracted by the idea of "a short novel about a young American leading a double life in college as a secret policeman." Such a novel might be somewhat less vulnerable to prefabricated literary patterning than *Vietnam* (father-son tensions, heterosexual-homosexual tensions, man-beast tensions, all framed in a "significant" Texas-Alaska polar symbology); but even so it would threaten to become an "idea for a novel novel" (a useful phrase adapted from Donald Hall) – something quite "made up" and possibly *forced.*

Toward the end of *The Armies of the Night,* Mailer writes of his feelings upon his release from jail after the demonstrations in Washington: "yes, in this resumption of the open air after twenty-four hours, no more, there was a sweet clean edge to the core of the substance of things – *a monumentally abstract remark which may be saved by the concrete observation* that the air was good in his lungs . . . [my italics]." The bard, perhaps wearied by labor too large and prolonged, has mauled a small bright human fact with the dull brutality of abstraction; and "Mailer," throwing off the robes of office, rebukes his alter ego for this crime against nature.

Mailer once wrote a story called "The Paper House," one of the conventionally "realistic" stories of the early 1950's that he does not take very seriously now, which is all about how reality takes its vengeance upon the criminal abstractionist. The setting is Japan. An arrogant, boorish, and selfish G.I. named Hayes is unsparingly loved by Yuriko, a geisha uncommonly endowed with dignity as well as tenderness. By night he nourishes upon her love. By day he is the thorough cynic: "crap" is what he calls the unhappy story of her family's misfortunes, her indenturing to training and service, and her final and staunch pride in earning the status of "first-class geisha." Crap: she is a common whore. He subconsciously wants to marry her, the natural concomitant in him of her unqualified love. But instead he drunkenly jeers at her: she is a common whore, and he will return to the States without her. When she responds by claiming him with increased vigor he strikes and strips her, brutally humiliating her before her peers and their clients. Later, when he meekly returns, she is as warm with him as ever, but sad and a bit withdrawn. What does this mean? She must go on a journey very soon, somewhat before his own departure for the States. Where? he persists. Why? What sort of journey? Finally he learns: because she, a first-class geisha, has been publicly dishonored by her lover, she will commit hari-kari. Crap! he cries in irritable disdain. He will speak no more of it. A whore is a whore! But through the days that follow, her familiar tender attentions are touched with silent grief. Though he does not deign to speak of her threat, inside he aches with dread. And on the appointed day he cannot hold himself back from going to her. He finds her dressed in white, "without ornament, and without makeup," pleased that he has come after all to say "Bye-bye." As she turns to go to her self-appointed justice, he catches her by the arm, crying, "You got to stop this. It's crap." "Crap-crap," says Yuriko in answer, giggling. And hidden all around, the other geishas echo, "Crap-crap." Hayes retreats, and the girls follow him, a massed march of laughing, bright-kimonoed angels of derision jeering the conquered bully through the town to the chorused tune of "Crap-crap, Crap-crap."

A memorably fine story in its own right (Mailer acknowledges indebtedness to Vance Bourjaily for the anecdote on which it is based) , it is also a model of Mailer's vision of marriage (in the soul-dimension Hayes and Yuriko are already "married") as the ultimate battleground of the laws of strife that govern love and sexuality, and in turn all of life. Alternatively turned on its side, upended, and inverted, "The Paper House" becomes a paradigm of the love-as-soulmaking-or-soulbreaking-combat themes of *The Deer Park*, "The Time of Her Time," and *An American Dream*. But it can also be read as a paradigm of the larger operations of a yet more ultimate law. In sharp contrast to his tender and humane buddy who narrates the story, Hayes is terrified of empathy. His is the naturally totalitarian temperament, bellowing, pounding, *forcing* reality to the shape of his belief. But Yuriko, whose unreasoning love frightens him into his worst brutality, *is* reality. The dignity of her otherness will not bend; she will not, finally, be forced. Her suavely just humiliation of her lover is so satisfying because it is a *natural* justice. A perfect illustration of the penalties which in the natural scheme of things are levied against unrepentant abstractionists who sin, through violence or neglect, against the actual.

This formula may provide one explanation of why it is that some people "can't read" Mailer any more, and why even those who can and do read him find themselves at times, especially when reading his fiction, fatigued, irritated, hankering after something which the apocalyptic apparatus of his imagination quite purposely extracts and draws off from his material so that no dilution will threaten the strong potion of his vision. Perhaps it is thanks to the just and beneficent workings of Yuriko's law that Mailer cannot finally succeed in this effort. Perhaps this explains why his best work, the work that moves as well as amazes, is his most "impure" – as in *The Deer Park*, where the mere presence of Charles Francis Eitel and Elena Esposito mocks, with the awesome poignant reality of their flawed selves and failed love, the unreality of Sergius O'Shaugnessy and Marion Faye, those stiff and faceless standard-bearers of the author's abstract redemptive "truth."

While Mailer has steadfastly refused to be apologetic about his journalism, he has equally steadfastly identified his highest goals as a writer with some major achievement as a novelist. In *The Armies of the Night* he is quite openly if good-humoredly annoyed by Robert Lowell's insistent praises of him as our greatest "journalist" at the same time he envies Lowell's quiet authority in the role of "poet." It is a fact, I think, that the large and responsive audience Mailer has now won at the close of the sixties would tend to agree, no doubt to the writer's chagrin, that his "best" work has been in nonfiction. In putting forth my own concurrence I would want to make clear that while I view *Barbary Shore* and *Why Are We in Vietnam?* as inferior achievements (they are "abstract" in my sense of the word: they busy themselves making points rather than peopling a world; and the mannerisms of their prose, portentous in one case, ranting in the other, are dubious compensation for this impoverishment) they nevertheless have interest and deserve respect in the total picture of Mailer's career as honorable attempts at experiment and innovation.

Granting the solid excellence — its truth of substance and feeling, as well as its art — of *The Naked and the Dead,* and the breathless virtuosity of *An American Dream,* only *The Deer Park* remains in the running for honors as a "great" novel. Its depth and breadth of imaginative engagement with our time, its acute and inclusive sensing of the way we live now, through deft selection of setting and symbol and deft portraiture of a dozen varied secondary characters that are real as well as symptomatic, make it impressive. But as we move toward the core of this book — the affair between Elena and Eitel — surely we move from the impressive into the field of force of something like "greatness." Eitel, the hero-gentleman demeaned by history, is a complex character of almost tangible reality; he has all the fullness of being that Fitzgerald could not finally give to Dick Diver. Elena, the soiled broad and dumb waif of petty disasters, is rich with an inner gift of instinctive warmth and natural dignity worthy of Cleopatra; she is one of the few great woman characters in American fiction after James. The delicate, tender persistence of Mailer's articulation of the life of their affair, its growth, flowering, deterioration, and crippled resolution, is rare and magnificent. It is the *real* "armature" of the book, despite Mailer's efforts to give that power to his prophets of new consciousness, Marion Faye and Sergius O'Shaugnessy. Because Sergius, like Lovett in *Barbary Shore*, seems neither intelligent nor sensitive nor good enough, nor even *visible* enough, to attract the friendship and confidence of a man like Eitel, we do not believe in him. But we cannot quite console ourselves by saying, with Lawrence, "Never trust the author, trust the tale," because we are distracted and fatigued as we read by the badgering of Mailer's forcing style of imagination – and the book's armature slows, finally, and falters. *The Deer Park*, one can say (Mailer's exactly opposite account of its shortcomings notwithstanding), was a potentially great novel flawed by an authorial excess of misled good intentions. It is perhaps yet another validation of Yuriko's law that what remains persistently alive in one's memory of *The Deer Park* is Eitel and Elena, and the real world, intimate and at large, of which they were the vital center.

In the middle 1950's Mailer professed a credo that would still seem to hold for him in the late 1960's:

I suppose that the virtue I should like most to achieve as a writer is to be genuinely disturbing . . . It is, I believe, the highest function a writer may serve, to see life (no matter by what means or form or experiment) as others do not see it, or only partially see it, and therefore open for the reader that literary experience which comes uniquely from the novel – the sense of having one's experience enlarged, one's perceptions deepened, and one's illusions about oneself rendered even more untenable. For me, this is the highest function of art, precisely that it is disturbing, that it does not let man rest, and therefore forces him so far as art may force anything to enlarge the horizons of his life.

It is clear that most of his work to date has been done in the light of this statement of principle, and it seems probable that it will continue to be, if only because it is the kind of principle that any serious novelist of whatever artistic or philosophic persuasion would be likely to subscribe to with dedication. But it could be argued that in his fiction, at least, Mailer has yet to write a book worthy of the strictest interpretation of his principle. If he eventually completes the multi-volume quasi-epic of neo-Joycean structure and Burroughs-*cum*-Tolstoian substance that he has been promising these many years, it probably will not be the novel, any more than his others have been, that fulfills the high aims of this credo. If he is to write a truly "great" novel, it will be the product of some new, subtler, and perhaps unimaginably humbler synthesis of the gifts for which he has now come to be appreciated. Perhaps he will learn something from his readers' obstinate tendency to prefer his nonfiction, where, with no sacrifice of his skills and all benefit to the power of his vision, he is happily mired in reality, hobbled to the facts of time, place, self, as to an indispensable spouse of flesh and blood who continually saves him from his other self that yearns toward wasteful flirtations with *Spiritus Mundi*. In any case, he will have to come to know truly, if in his own way, the "Thou" to which the "I" of Martin Buber's world is inexorably wedded, and he will have to find his own style of that "negative capability" which Keats identified as the root of true imagination.

Perhaps Mailer would dismiss such cavils as typical of the solemnly moribund mentality of official literary criticism. And yet he might be reminded that the newly respectful concern with his work, represented even by such exceptions as these, is the natural harvest, sought or not, of his maverick persistence in his calling—and for Mailer writing has always been, literally, a "calling"—despite the years of criticism's ignorant undervaluation of him. He has finally forced criticism, which once dismissed him as a sensationalist barbarian egomaniac who couldn't write, to eat its own words, salted and spiced with the true savor of his actual achievements. Criticism has been made to confess at last that Mailer is a symbolist and mythmaker, the alchemy of his imagination being capable of turning excrement, madness, and perversion into lambent revelations of the condition of man and God; that he is a true intellectual – acute, sophisticated, and dead serious in his probing criticisms of the life of his time; that he is an extraordinary prose stylist in the big-voiced Amercan tradition of Melville and Faulkner; and that he is fortunately endowed, as most apocalyptics are not, with the easing human graces of wit and humor. Even such a book as *Advertisements for Myself,* which at the time of its publication so outraged and embarrassed the critics with its naked revelations of its author's wounds and vanities, has now come to seem, in the manner of Fitzgerald's "Crack-Up" essays, a nobly original undertaking of self-definition, moving in content and daring in execution. *Advertisements* represents the invention, furthermore, of a new form (let's call it, to borrow a current term that has been misapplied elsewhere, the "nonfiction novel"), a form that has since served him well in *The Presidential Papers, Cannibals and Christians,* and *The Armies of the Night,* and will no doubt continue to do so.

But if his readers continue to feel, with some validity, that in the light of "the tradition" Mailer is not the finished and fully responsible writer-as-*artist* that many of his peers are, it has become easier lately to answer with equal validity that he nevertheless satisfies again and again, as they do not, by surprise. Where critics once measured his failings by the more finished accomplishments of his peers, it is now possible to suggest measurement of the shortcomings of his peers by citing the obstinate vigor of Mailer's restless creativity. For example: we are now capable of thinking (however our words are chosen to express the thought) of Mailer's imaginative ingenuity, that it is never so depthless as Barth's can be; of his ambitious fluency of expression, that it is never so hollow and self-serving as Styron's penchant for "style" can become; of his ideas and his humanity, that they do not seem borrowed or "literary" as do, respectively, a large portion of Bellow's and Malamud's.

It may be that Mailer has succeeded in enlarging a little the range of literature in his time, and that in so doing he has measurably modified our view of "the tradition." What is at least certain is that simply by persisting in being what he must be, writing as he must write, he has taught many of his critics to think more justly about his work, to respond more accurately to it. And a friendly commentator, taking all these facts and speculations into account, could hope that the work Mailer does in the future will fully justify what a young English instructor, whose equivalent only a few years ago would have turned the corners of his mouth down at the mere mention of Mailer's name, said to me only days before these sentences were written – "He's about the best we've got going for us now."

Selected Bibliography

Works of Norman Mailer

NOVELS AND COLLECTIONS OF SHORT STORIES

The Naked and the Dead. New York: Holt, Rinehart, and Winston, 1948.
Barbary Shore. New York: Holt, Rinehart, and Winston, 1951.
The Deer Park. New York: Putnam, 1955; Dial, 1967.
An American Dream. New York: Dial, 1965.
The Short Fiction of Norman Mailer. New York: Dell (paperback), 1967.
Why Are We in Vietnam? New York: Putnam, 1967.

OTHER PROSE

Advertisements for Myself. New York: Putnam, 1959.
The Presidential Papers. New York: Putnam, 1963.
Cannibals and Christians. New York: Dial, 1966.
The Armies of the Night. New York: New American Library, 1968.
The Bullfight, a Photographic Narrative with Text by Norman Mailer. New York: CBS Legacy Collection Book, distributed by Macmillan, 1967.

PLAY

The Deer Park. New York: Dial, 1967.

POEMS

Deaths for the Ladies, and Other Disasters. New York: Putnam, 1962.

CURRENT AMERICAN REPRINTS

Advertisements for Myself. New York: Berkley. $.95.
An American Dream. New York: Dell. $.95.
Barbary Shore, with Introduction by Norman Podhoretz. New York: Universal Library (Grosset). $1.95. New York: Signet (New American Library). $.75.
Cannibals and Christians. New York: Dell. $.95.
The Deer Park. New York: Berkley. $.75. New York: Signet. $.75.
The Deer Park (play). New York: Dell. $.95.
The Idol and the Octopus (original). New York: Dell. $.95.
The Naked and the Dead. New York: Signet. $.95. New York: Holt, Rinehart,

and Winston (edited by Chester E. Eisinger). $2.95. New York: Modern Library (Random House). $2.45.

The Short Fiction of Norman Mailer (original). New York: Dell. $.95.

The White Negro (original). San Francisco: City Lights Book Shop. $.75.

Why Are We in Vietnam? New York: Berkley. $.95.

Critical and Biographical Material

Aldridge, John W. *Time to Murder and Create*. New York: McKay, 1966.

Blotner, Joseph. *The Political Novel in America*. Austin and London: University of Texas Press, 1966.

Breit, Harvey. *The Writer Observed*. Cleveland and New York: World, 1956.

Corrington, J. W. "An American Dream," *Chicago Review*, 18:58–66 (Summer 1965).

Dienstfrey, Harris. "Norman Mailer," in *On Contemporary Literature*, edited by Richard Kostelanetz. New York: Avon, 1964.

Eisinger, Chester E. *Fiction of the Fifties*. Chicago: University of Chicago Press, 1963.

Glicksberg, Charles I. "Norman Mailer: The Angry Young Novelist in America," *Wisconsin Studies in Contemporary Literature*, 1:25–34 (Winter 1960).

Harper, Howard M., Jr. *Desperate Faith*. Chapel Hill: University of North Carolina Press, 1967.

Hoffman, Frederick J. "Norman Mailer and the Heart of the Ego: Some Observations on Recent American Literature," *Wisconsin Studies in Contemporary Literature*, 1:5–12 (Fall 1960).

Ludwig, Jack. *Recent American Novelists*. Minneapolis: University of Minnesota Press, 1962.

Millgate, Michael. *American Social Fiction: James to Cozzens*. Edinburgh and London: Oliver and Boyd, 1964.

"Norman Mailer: An Interview," in *Writers at Work: The Paris Review Interviews* (third series), with Introduction by Alfred Kazin. New York: Viking, 1967.

"*Playboy* Interview: Norman Mailer," *Playboy*, 15:69–84 (January 1968).

Podhoretz, Norman. "Norman Mailer: The Embattled Vision," *Partisan Review*, 26:371–91 (Summer 1959).

Poirier, Richard. "T. S. Eliot and the Literature of Waste," *New Republic*, 156:19–25 (May 20, 1967).

Schrader, George A. "Norman Mailer and the Despair of Defiance," *Yale Review*, 51:267–80 (Winter 1962).

Toback, James. "Norman Mailer Today," *Commentary*, 44:68–76 (October 1967).

Schulz, Max F. "Mailer's Divine Comedy," *Contemporary Literature*, 9:36–57 (Winter 1968).

Trilling, Diana. "The Radical Moralism of Norman Mailer," in *The Creative Present*, edited by Nona Balakian and Charles Simmons. Garden City, N.Y.: Doubleday, 1963.

Volpe, Edmund L. "James Jones – Norman Mailer," in *Contemporary American Novelists*, edited by Harry T. Moore. Carbondale: Southern Illinois University Press, 1964.

Wagenheim, Allen J. "Square's Progress: *An American Dream*," *Critique*, 10:45–68 (Winter 1968).

Weber, Brom. "A Fear of Dying: Norman Mailer's *An American Dream*," *Hollins Critic*, 2:1–6 (1965).

Wood, Margery. "Norman Mailer and Nathalie Sarraute: A Comparison of Existentialist Novels," *Minnesota Review*, 6:67–72 (Spring 1966).